Reasons to Reason

Reasons to Reason

*Defending the Faith
Is Good for Christians*

NANCY A. ALMODOVAR

RESOURCE *Publications* • Eugene, Oregon

REASONS TO REASON
Defending the Faith Is Good for Christians

Copyright © 2021 Nancy A. Almodovar. All rights reserved. Except for brief quotations in critical publications or reviews, no part of this book may be reproduced in any manner without prior written permission from the publisher. Write: Permissions, Wipf and Stock Publishers, 199 W. 8th Ave., Suite 3, Eugene, OR 97401.

Resource Publications
An Imprint of Wipf and Stock Publishers
199 W. 8th Ave., Suite 3
Eugene, OR 97401

www.wipfandstock.com

PAPERBACK ISBN: 978-1-6667-0604-8
HARDCOVER ISBN: 978-1-6667-0605-5
EBOOK ISBN: 978-1-6667-0606-2

07/12/21

To my husband Bobby, thank you for your encouragement and amazing love toward me.

For Christians everywhere who have never thought to study Apologetics, I trust that at the end of this book you will have recognized the benefits for you the believer and are encouraged to study Apologetics further.

The Christian life is an apologetic.
—Rev. Craig Kellerman, Faith Lutheran Church (LCMS)

Contents

Preface | ix
Introduction | xiii
1 Earnestly Contend | 1
2 Experience or Evidence? | 11
3 Educated & Equipped | 26
4 Encouraged & Excited | 35
5 Endurance | 41
6 Epilogue | 49
Bibliography | 51

Preface

For it is the mark of a fair man to prove and attest what he proclaims and says.

– Martin Luther

Beloved, although I was very eager to write to you about our common salvation, I found it necessary to write appealing to you to contend for the faith that was once for all delivered to the saints . . . building yourselves up in your most holy faith. (Jude 3 & 20)

A FUNNY THING HAPPENED as I began studying how and why to defend the Christian faith; my own faith grew and was strengthened. As a Lutheran I understand that God has chosen to work through the Means of Grace. One of these Means is the Word of God. However, St. Paul reminds us in Rom 10 that unless someone proclaims that Jesus died, was buried, and rose again from the dead for the forgiveness of sins, no one is going to be saved. You see, we need to speak up. That can be scary. Still, God tells us in His Word (1 Pet 3) that we are to have a reason/answer for the hope that is within. That's where Apologetics comes in.

Studying Apologetics as the focus of my degrees was not my intent when I returned to higher education. In fact, I did not, even as a Christian, know what it meant. However, upon learning that Apologetics means to give a reason and defense for the faith, I jumped into the field full throttle and haven't stopped yet (though when I was a Calvinist the cold waters of bad theology attempted to douse the flames, but converting to Lutheranism ignited them further). Other than those years as a Dutch Reformed/Calvinist I haven't really looked back (see *The Accidental Lutheran* for why I stopped doing Apologetics as a Calvinist).

Then came a global situation (2020) which opened up a way to teach Apologetics online. With so many on lockdown from the virus, I thought why not visit with friends/family and teach them to defend the Christian faith in a world very frightened by the strong possibility of sickness and death. What happened is that believers were learning that our faith is not a "blind faith" or "unreasonable" and that we have solid, objective, and documented evidential proofs for the Christian faith. These lessons lead to their own faith being strengthened and built up.

Jude writes to his parish that they need to contend for the faith against those who are either false teachers and those outside the faith. Reading through his epistle, the reader discovers that at the close of the letter, Jude is encouraging Christians to build themselves up in their "most holy faith." I can't help but think that there is a correlation between learning the facts of the Christian faith in order to defend it to unbelievers, skeptics, or false teachers, and the effect on our personal faith. When we learn to defend the faith we see more clearly that our great God strengthens, reinforces and builds up our faith even more.

This book is not about how to do Apologetics (although I will go through the evidence of the Christian faith) but rather how preparing a defense has unintended benefits for Christians. We gain from learning, more and more, all that God has given us in our preparation and so even if you are not engaged in Apologetics, it is good for you! It is my hope that as you read and understand the many benefits which come from preparing to answer for your faith, you will then become engaged in Apologetics with those in your social circle. Just imagine the everlasting impact of answering the questions of those who do not yet know Jesus as the Forgiver of sins and Conqueror of sin, death, and the devil for themselves.

May God graciously build you up in the faith as you earnestly contend for the truth once delivered to the saints. Amen.

Introduction

> "We see that He has overwhelmed us with unspeakable, eternal treasures by His Son and the Holy Spirit."[1]

IN A RECENT VIDEO conference with a pastor, we were discussing some upcoming topics for articles I was ask to write for the Utah/Idaho Lutheran Women's Missionary League (LWML). As we chatted we began to discuss the benefits that studying and doing Apologetics offers to the Christian as they are defending the faith. That conversation reminded me of what I learned over fifteen years ago in my first Apologetics class at Trinity Theological Seminary under Dr. John Warwick Montgomery: Apologetics builds Christians in their faith. This book is about those benefits and how you can grow in your faith as you study defending the Christian faith.

While this book is not about styles of Apologetics, and there are many variants of defending the faith, it is about you, the Christian, and growing in grace and knowledge. It is about why one should study Apologetics and how it will benefit your own walk with God. This is not a how-to book on doing Apologetics but instead an encouragement for you to get going in defending the faith while at the same time building you up in our most holy faith.

As I was writing my previous two books, *Creedal Apologetics* and *They Were Eyewitnesses*, in the video class I offer weekly, one gentleman said that Apologetics has helped his own faith to grow.

1. Dau, *Concordia*, 401.

Introduction

One question often asked by believers is why we are Christians? Luther wrote:

"What sort of a God do you have? What do you know about Him?" Our answer should be something like this: "This is my God: first, the Father, who has created Heaven and earth. Besides this One only, I regard nothing else as God. For there is no one else who could create Heaven and earth."[2] Since this is who our God is, it is only right that when learning to defend the faith our walk with God is strengthened.

---

2. Dau, *Concordia*, 399.

1

Earnestly Contend

Beloved, although I was very eager to write to you about our common salvation, I found it necessary to write appealing to you to contend for the faith that was once for all delivered to the saints. . . . But you, beloved, building yourselves up in your most holy faith . . . (Jude 3 & 20)

One modern scholar, T. R. Glover of Cambridge University declared that the Christians out-thought, out-lived, and out-died the adherents of the non-Christian religions. The primary source of the appeal of Christianity was Jesus—His incarnation, His life, His crucifixion, and His resurrection.[1]

I REMEMBER IN ONE of the very first lectures by Dr. Montgomery at Trinity Theological Seminary via their online courses, that he said Apologetics, in a sense, comes back to us Christians with great benefits. In recalling this advice, I've often called it the boomerang

1. Latourette, "Christianity Through the Ages."

effect of Apologetics: It comes back to us with more reasons to believe the Scriptures. As Christians engage in the study of Apologetics we grow in our own faith as we learn about the evidence and eyewitness testimony God has given us in His Word. Dr. Montgomery often spoke of how knowing the facts of the text, understanding that the apostles were eyewitnesses, comprehending the vastness of fulfilled prophecies and their implications to truth, were just some of the benefits Christians gained when contending for the faith. He also said that Christians should be widely read on contemporary issues as well as archaeological and historical matters. With this preparation Christians can compete in the marketplace of ideas with that one historical event that changed the world: The physical death, burial, and resurrection of Jesus for the forgiveness of our sins.

My own pastor, Rev. Craig Kellerman, said to me, "The Christian life is an apologetic." When Christians are living out their faith, attending the divine service, and being served by God through the Sacraments of Word and the Lord's Supper, through daily prayer, study, and reading the Scriptures it actually is apologetical. Let me explain.

Apologetics is about giving an answer or a defense of the faith. When we engage in those things listed above it gives our own hearts and minds an answer for the faith. This, then, builds up our faith and equips us to respond to the questions of both inquirers and skeptics. When we respond to the skeptics or the person truly wanting to know what we believe and why, then we are earnestly contending for the faith. For Christians, having the answers to their questions shows that you did not just become a Christian because of your feelings (maybe you started out that way) but there are facts and reasons to believe based upon the eyewitness testimony we have been given in the New Testament.

Reading the Epistle of Jude you get the sense that Jude is talking about defending the faith from attacks within and without the church. Right at the start he reminds Christians that they must contend for the faith once delivered to them. He exhorts them to come against the arguments of those sowing discord in the church and also to those who deny Jesus. The end of his letter is where he encourages them to build up themselves in the faith. One way to do that is to learn to defend the faith against the charges of the unbeliever and skeptic. However, sometimes we must defend the faith from those in the church, as Martin Luther wrote, "who by deceit or sword would wrest the kingdom from Your Son and bring to naught all He has done."[2] Since the days of the Apostles there have been those who would want to sow deceit and discord into the church. Christians who know what they believe and why then have the ability to earnestly contend for the faith and teach the erring believer what is faithful and true to God's Word.

Apologetics reminds us that the Christian faith is founded on fact and not fiction. It informs us of the testimonial and documentary evidences that God has gifted the church through His written Word and all the archaeological proof of the history contained therein as well. Apologetics shouldn't been thought to be only for the theologians and pastors but that the everyday believer would contend for the faith. In the end, Jude reminds us to build ourselves up in our most holy faith.

Then we read of St. Peter's exhortation to have a defense ready for when you are questioned (1 Pet 3). However, this is not directed at the professors or pastors, but to the parishioners in the pew. That's you and me. We, everyday Christians, must be prepared to answer for our faith.

However, the benefits we receive back by doing that preparation is innumerable. That's where this book comes in. Do Apologetics scare you? Are you wondering, as I did the first time I heard the term, "What is Apologetics?" Do you wonder why it is so necessary that the Apostles define it and encourage us to be ready? Over and over, when I teach Apologetics or engage in the defense of the faith with the person of either no religion or some newfound "spirituality," I find that my faith grows . . . even if I get all jumbled trying to answer their questions (Apologetics). It is the benefits of Apologetics that I want to show in this book so that you will see

---

2. Commission on Worship of the Lutheran Church—Missouri Synod, *Lutheran Service Book*, 655.

them. God always tells us to do something because it is good for us. Quite simply we can say, Apologetics is good for you! Therefore, since Apologetics is a tool within the toolbox of Evangelism so that we may proclaim Jesus Christ who lived, died, was buried, and rose again for the forgiveness of all our sins, perhaps we should get a little into the what it is so that we can then move on to the why's of defending the Christian faith. The how-to of Apologetics I have left to what I have written in the books *Creedal Apologetics*, *They Were Eyewitnesses*, and *Nothing Else Matters*. This book is concerned with why Christians everywhere and at all times should be engaged with friends, family, coworkers, neighbors, and others within their social circle answering their questions about the faith.

WHAT IS APOLOGETICS?

It is key to understanding the biblical use of this term before understanding how it applies in our Christian life every single day. In 1 Pet 3:15, the Apostle writes: "In your hearts honor Christ the Lord as holy, always being prepared to make a defense to anyone who asks you for a reason for the hope that is in you; yet do it with gentleness and respect. . . ."

The word defense is a Greek word transliterated into English as "apologia"—apologetic. Variations of this meaning are as follows and each places the weight upon evidence or documented testimonials (we call them the Gospels and Acts specifically and generally the New Testament): a verbal defense, a speech given in defense, a well-reasoned statement or argument. We may phrase it this way: It is giving the skeptic and seeker evidence offered in making the case for the truth of Christianity.

Apologetics is simply a tool in your evangelism toolbox. That's your go-to equipment that helps you to share the Good News that Jesus died and rose again for the forgiveness of our sins. Evangelism mostly happens over a period of time where you may be just a link in a long chain until the unbeliever or skeptic comes to true faith in Jesus Christ. On the rare occasion, they may hear and immediately believe, but most of the time it doesn't happen that quickly. In fact, for the unchurched, they may have heard the Good News before and you were at the end of that long chain.

Mostly you are engaged in Apologetics without even knowing when you share why you believe. Apologetics is not this big scary craft that is left for the professionals. Every Christian, with a little bit of training, lots of prayer, and tons of love for others, can learn to use this tool in its various forms.

Christians, must remember that one of our many vocations is as ambassadors for Christ (2 Cor 5:20). We are to make our case for the unbeliever to turn to Jesus Christ, the crucified and risen One. We are to call them to repent and believe. First, this means answering their questions and then giving them the Gospel (Jesus died, was buried, and rose again for the forgiveness of all our sins).

It also means understanding their questions. This entails studying ahead of time various questions they may have so that you can offer adequate and reasonable answers. Second Tim 2:15 instructs us to be approved (Gk. *dokimon*: genuine after being tested) workers who correctly interpret the Scriptures. It is our responsibility to study the Scriptures and know what they teach.

In our daily vocations we strive to do and be the best we can. The same must be applied to our Christian life. We should be studying the Word of God so that we can answer their questions with the Word of God. Never forget that it is the "Gospel which is the power of God unto salvation" (Rom 1:16–17). We are not making philosophical arguments. In the Formula of Concord, the writers state that which Luther warned: we are not to use philosophical terms because they will result in a "great potential for needless offense, confusion, and misunderstanding."[3] Therefore, we must bring them the Word of God.

When you go to do a task or a job given to you, if you stood there talking about all the possibilities or theories but never actually did the work, you would not be called back. Therefore, we too, since our Christian life is an apologetic, must do the things necessary to fulfill that vocation too. Whether a mom, dad, office manager, teacher, plumber or cabinet maker, nurse, electrician, or

---

3. Dau, *Concordia*, 471.

writer, you will have opportunities to answer their questions. Your responsibility is to avail yourself of all the tools the Christian faith offers to help you adequately answer their questions.

Since I'm married to a master cabinet maker I've learned over the decades that each tool has its purpose. The same goes with Apologetics. We are wise to both learn these tools and the skill to use them at the right time so that we have a defense ready (that means you know both what it is and how to use it). Apologetics is similar to actual tools. Let me explain.

Pliers: Used to pull old or crooked nails out. Apologetics pulls out the wrong ideas (fiction and feelings) the unbeliever may have about Jesus, the Gospel, or the Bible.

A square: This tool makes sure the corners are accurate so when you are finished building it's not crooked. In other words, it straightens out some things that the enquirer may have almost right but still a bit off. In love and gentleness we correct the false teachings and square them with the Word of God.

Hammer: This drives the nail home to hold something together or up. In Apologetics, this is the driving point of the Gospel: Jesus died, was buried, and rose again according to the Scriptures.

Measuring tape: This keeps us in line while working, measuring out the correct dimensions. As we seek to respond to their questions we desire to remain in line with the Word of God giving our responses and not our opinions. If we built something just by opinion, saying, "looks good there," would we ever trust it to be true and trustworthy? Probably not. We want what we are building to be safe and correctly figured. How can we offer less when dealing with the eternal destination of the person? We can't and shouldn't. Therefore, the plumb line for Christians is the Scripture. Theologians call it the canon of Scripture, meaning the "collection of books that form the original and authoritative written rule of the faith and practice of the Christian Church."[4]

Saws: Cutting parts to fit together is what carpenters and cabinet makers do. They look at a piece of wood, check them for being straight and flush, choose the best looking wood and after

---

4. Smith, "Canon of Scripture."

measuring twice they cut once. What is the saw for the Christian? It really is the skill to not only be a skilled, tested, and approved worker for the Lord but it reminds us to "orthotomeō" or correctly cut without distortion, the Word of God. We are to know the Word of God sufficiently to be able to show from various texts what the Bible teaches and then apply it to their questions. This application may be the part where many Christians get lost or feel inadequate to the task. However, you are not. If you've learned the Apostles' Creed you have the key parts of the faith already in your mind and heart. Trust the Holy Spirit to pull up what is specifically needed to cut through their excuses and bring them to true faith and repentance in the one who died, was buried, and rose again for the forgiveness of their sins.

Apologetics then is simply a tool you can use to answer their questions about the Christian faith. The beauty of Apologetics is that these tools I just compared it to above actually work in our lives too. When we study Apologetics the wrong teachings from scripture get pulled out. It aligns our belief with what the Bible plainly says, just like a square in cabinetry does. It hammers home for believers that Jesus died, was buried, and rose again according to the Scriptures for *my* sins, for *your* sins. When we hear the Gospel it builds our faith in Jesus Christ the only Son, our Lord. In other words, Apologetics is a faith-building tool for Christians that is good for you!

PROCLAIM GENTLY WITH BOLDNESS

The Bible has given us all the proofs we need to remove their objections (hurdles, stumbling blocks) to eventually bring the unbeliever to the Door of Salvation, Jesus Christ. On the outside of the door it says, "The Spirit and the Bride say, 'Come.' And let the one who hears say, 'Come.' And let the one who is thirsty come; let the one who desires take the water of life without price" (Rev 22:17) and on the inside "chosen from in Him (Jesus Christ) before the foundation of the world" (Eph 1:4). Only God can bring them conviction and convert them but He uses us to proclaim the Gospel to them.

Scripture says that we are to "speak truth in love." That is actually quite a tall order. When we think of proclaiming truth we may think of a bullhorn. However, Scripture is talking about crouching down, sitting next to the person or child, and "become all things to all people, that by all means I might save some" (1 Cor 9:22).

WHAT APOLOGETICS IS NOT

Apologetics, defending the faith, is not about who wins the argument. It is about removing their objections to believing the Gospel so that they must confront the truth and either bend the knee in loving submission to Christ or walk away into an eternity apart from His love. It is about removing those hurdles with love and gentleness (1 Pet 2:15) and proclaiming to them the only One in whom we have true hope.

Apologetics is not about bringing in your own doctrinal preferences nor your testimony. The Gospel is not a story about you. It is not how horrific you were prior to conversion or how incredible your testimony is. Nowhere are we told that our experiences prove the Christian faith and to do so debilitates a proper Gospel proclamation by relying upon the same faulty ground as every other cult and world religion, as argued in the chapter on other religions.

It is simply giving an answer for the hope that you have and that answer is Jesus who died, was buried, and rose again according to the Scriptures.

There are many hurdles you will come up against. For example, they may not even know who Jesus is. They may wonder if there is a God. The problem of pain usually comes up and you have to talk to them about why there is sickness and death in our world. You will often come up against their challenges to the validity of the Bible and who wrote it. Finally, one of the go-to responses is that they see the hypocrisy of Christians and want no part of that. Each of these can be dealt with, lovingly and steadily, by engaging in Apologetics. As each objection/hurdle is removed, you bring them one step closer to the door of our salvation, Jesus Christ.

As you love your neighbor by engaging in Apologetics prayerfully, God will work through His Word by the power of His Holy Spirit. Where you lack skill, He still works. Where you get flustered or frustrated, God is patient and kind, not willing that any should perish. We rely upon the Holy Spirit who works through the Means of Grace to grant saving faith and one of those means is the proclaimed Word of God, the Bible.

Now that you know what Apologetics is and isn't, let's move on to how Christians benefit from preparing to and then defending the faith. Jude, after the majority of his letter is about contending for the Christian faith from those who would bring in pernicious error and heresy, encourages believers to build themselves up in the faith. Jude reminds his parishioners that in the last days there will be scoffers, skeptics, and those who try to sow discord. His remedy for the believers is that they build themselves up in the faith. This is done by attending the preaching and reading of God's Word at the divine service, getting to Bible studies, availing oneself of the Means of Grace in the Lord's Supper (baptism for the new convert and their family), and studying to show yourself an "approved worker rightly dividing the Word of God" (2 Tim 3:16–17) and ready for every good work (Titus 3:2).

When Peter says to have a defense ready he means to be prepared, which means we should be equipped to give a reasonable, rational, objective reason for our faith. We do not have a blind faith made up of cunningly devised fables, but the truth through which alone is the forgiveness of sins and life everlasting. As we become better prepared, equipped with God's Word and promise, He builds up our own faith and strengthens it in various ways. Since the Christian life is an apologetic it is important that every Christian everywhere learn the basic skills and thereby receive the benefits for their own faith as they also learn to defend the faith in the upside down world around them.

Studying Apologetics is not just for the pastor or professor but for the one who professes their faith in Jesus Christ who died, was buried, and rose again. It is a tool in your evangelism toolbox that every Christian should be acquainted with and skilled to use. This is not a subject for the professionals but for the people of God. Just as you learned certain skills for the vocation God has placed you in, so too, Christians must have the tools needs to earnestly contend for the faith.

2

Experience or Evidence?

How did you become a Christian? Why are you a Christian? What convinced you Christianity was the religion to follow? Why do you believe in Jesus? Do you really believe in a god? What about evolution? Where do we go when we die? I heard Jesus didn't really exist. Is that true? I heard that Constantine put the Bible together. Is that correct? Who wrote the Bible?

These are just a few of the questions you may be asked by your friends, family, neighbors, and others in your social circle. As you can read, some take a bit more time to answer. However, the question does not matter. It is our answer that does. The Apostles, in every situation they were in, had a reasonable answer for their faith. By reasonable I mean one with reason and evidence to present when they proclaimed and defended the Christian faith. In fact, Luke tells us that the Apostle Paul would go to the synagogue for three Sabbath days in a row and "reasoned with them from the Scriptures, explaining and proving that it was necessary for the Christ to suffer and to rise from the dead"(Acts 17:2–3). Notice that St. Paul did not give them his testimony of his personal conversion on the road to Damascus. (Yes, he'd begin with that later at his trial but mostly he ditches the personal testimony and goes straight to the facts of the death and resurrection of Jesus.)

Many of these questions, at the top of the chapter, tend to rely upon our experience. However, personal experience is subjective and not provable. So, we Christians need to leave our personal conversion experiences and get to the heart of the matter: the life, death, burial, and resurrection of Jesus, according to the Scriptures (1 Cor 15:1-4). I've written about this quite often in my recent blogs posts and in the book *They Were Eyewitnesses* so if you want to learn the apostolic style of proclamation and defending the faith, check that out. Instead, here I want to focus on the benefits of this for the believer.

Why should I have a defense ready? First and foremost because God commands that we do. He tells us, through the Apostle Peter, to have an answer ready when they ask why your faith is in Jesus Christ. Why do you believe? Why are you a Christian? How do you know the Bible is true?

When you study the Christian faith you begin to learn better what you do believe and why. Studying of Apologetics involves studying the Scriptures. It means looking at the evidence that Peter, John, Paul, Stephen (the Deacon), Luke, Mark, Matthew, and others give us in the Word of God. It means knowing how to draw from a wealth of documentary testimonies and use them at the right time in the right way.

That's a great reason to study but how does that help you? The moment you begin to see that there are reasons for your faith you begin to understand that God has not left us with a blind faith but instead with an anchor that is sure and solid. You begin to realize that you are not grasping at vapor or some uncertain hopeful future. Instead, you have solid, rock solid footing underneath you on which you can stand stable and secure.

Studying Apologetics builds you up. If you think of it like a brick wall, the doctrines of our faith are the cornerstone and the bricks. Apologetics is the cement, the mortar that goes in between them and fixing them so they remain stable, solid, and secure.

In my #ApologeticsTogether Zoom classes (see Lutherangirl.org for more information on how to join these free classes) a young woman said this to me, "Before your class, when answering questions about my Christian faith, I always felt like I was bringing a knife to a gunfight. Not anymore. I know how to answer for my faith. I know what I believe and why." This is not an uncommon response for those who begin to learn Apologetics. Their own faith and ability to share/proclaim Christ to others is strengthened, becoming surer in evangelism.

Believers must emphasize that Christianity is not just one experience among many but is the only way of salvation and founded on the fact of the birth, ministry, miracles, death, and resurrection given by the evangelists who were actual eyewitnesses of these events.[1] Focusing upon a subjective presentation, we do not offer the world a better way but simply another one that may or may not give them inner peace. This system does indeed bankrupt the Gospel message and brings it to an equal level with all other false religions.

The answer to this is that every believer must move quickly from testifying of their own personal experience, away from their own denominational peculiarities and subjective experiences on to the Gospel of Christ and Him crucified and risen again. The reason for defending the faith is to bring the unbeliever to the foot of the cross and to the point where they must choose to believe or reject Jesus Christ. Believers of all theological backgrounds must focus back onto the Gospel. As Netland writes,

> In our witness to an unbelieving world primacy must always be given the simple, direct, Spirit-anointed proclamation of the Gospel... where appropriate, such witness should also be supplemented by informed and sensitive response to criticism and questions and demonstration of why one should accept the claims of Christian faith.[2]

Nowhere are we told that our experiences prove the Christian faith and to do so debilitates a proper Gospel proclamation by relying upon the same faulty ground as every other cult and world religion.

---

1. Greenleaf, "Testimony of the Apostles."
2. Netland, *Evangelical Apologetics*, 297.

What then should a Gospel defense and proclamation look like? Perhaps we would do well to read and study the sermons found in the Book of Acts and have the Apostles teach us. In total ten of the sermons found in the Book of Acts given by the original Apostles and St. Paul will be utilized to see what and whom the focus was of preaching and evangelizing. Do they focus on the ecstatic gifts, the miracles they did in the name of Jesus or do they zero in on the verifiable resurrection of Him from the dead? If the latter, then perhaps our Pentecostal and Charismatic brothers and sisters will listen to the Word of God as their teacher and regain a robust evangel about the resurrection rather than their personal experiences or charismata.

Dr. Montgomery has often referred to one purpose of Apologetics as removing the hurdles on the road to the House of Salvation. Keeping this analogy in mind, if we think of our personal testimony as the first stone on that cobble path, one never stays there when inviting others into our home. We walk off of that first stone and onto the next and so on until we read that Door of Salvation, which on the outside reads, "Whosoever will may enter." The path to that door is through the proclamation of the Gospel; the life, death, and resurrection of Jesus based upon the truths the Evangelists told us, actually "occurred within their own personal knowledge" and recorded for us in verifiable eyewitness documentation.[3]

Testimony may be a starting point but our own experiences pale in verifiable comparison to the proofs God has given us in His Word. Testimony may get the conversation going but believers must move quickly to the eyewitness accounts of the resurrection because that is the culminating point of the Gospel: forgiveness of sins because Jesus rose again for our justification (Rom 4:25). Testimonies, no matter how dramatic, will not bring life and salvation. God has told us that life and salvation are given through Jesus Christ who died and rose again for all people (Acts 4:12; Titus 2:11).

---

3. Greenleaf, "Testimony of the Apostles."

This subjective style of Apologetics does nothing for a true Gospel presentation and opens it up to rejection based on feelings and emotions. The modern idea that "what is true for you may not be true for me" relies upon subjectivism. However, the Gospel is objective true and therefore, what is true for me is most definitely true for you. This chapter will work on recovering the objective truth of the Gospel so that they may present to others the facts of God's Word, apart from their feelings or emotional experiences. Through looking at the focus of the sermons from the Book of Acts, it is the hope that those with a more subjective gospel, which results in a feelings/experience based proclamation, will return to that which the Apostles and early church declared: an objective truth that was validated by eyewitnesses given to the church in the Scriptures.

Counter to popular opinion among many evangelicals Christianity is not based upon your experience, your feelings, or some direct message from God in your heart or mind. While Christianity does not reject that at times your feelings will swell with joy, it also teaches us that conviction of sin will bring down any euphoria quickly. Christianity based upon happy, joyful, exuberant emotions is not the Christianity of history nor of the Bible. There is no doubt that the individual may feel something in the divine service, after absolution or partaking of the true body and blood of Christ, the faith is not based upon feelings but upon the objective truth that God has said, "I forgive you of your sins." God works from the outside first and then inwardly. However, evangelicals have flipped the order that God has given in His Word and have made even the proclamation of the Gospel one based upon whether it feels good. Luther reminded the Church, which at that time was steeped in an inner focus for assurance of salvation, that God always works through outward means, Extra Nos, first and then inwardly changes the person (Intra Nos).[4] That order is never to be confused and yet, the subjectivism of Pentecostalism has turned this order, and the Gospel, completely upside down with feet in the air and head in the sand.

4. Pelikan, *Luther's Works*, 40.

> The Presentation is of the Gospel not your particular denomination or theological system.
>
> —Dr. John Warwick Montgomery,
> Strasbourg France (2019)
> International Academy of Apologetics,
> Evangelism and Human Rights

For many of the evangelicals I grew up with, Apologetics seems quite unnecessary. Rather, we should just share what God has done for us and encourage them to make a decision. The idea for the Pentecostal is that by trying to defend the faith we are replacing the work of the Holy Spirit. We are trying to use human reasoning to save them. However, the Scriptures teach us to use various tools in proclaiming and defending the faith. Counseling, evangelism, whether large or small scale and Apologetics are all utilized by the Holy Spirit to bring a person to faith. Whether Pentecostal or other denomination, believers agree that reliance upon the Holy Spirit is critical for it is He alone who convicts the world of sin, unrighteousness, and judgment. Only He can bring new birth to the one who is dead in sin.

In *Scaling the Secular City*, J. P. Moreland encourages even those within his charismatic circles to overcome their objections to using Apologetics as one tool in the work of evangelism. He writes, "Apologetics is a ministry designed to help unbelievers over some intellectual obstacles and believers to remove doubts that hinder spiritual growth."[5] He likens the use of Apologetics with the use of the sermon in this vein. Further he writes,

> Apologetics can help remove obstacles to faith and thus aid unbelievers in embracing the gospel. Certainly the Holy Spirit must be involved in drawing men to Christ. But a preacher is not absolved of the responsibility of preparing his sermon just because the Spirit must apply the Word of God to the lives of his listeners. In the same way, ambassadors for Christ are not excused from the

---

5. Moreland, *Scaling the Secular City*, 11.

responsibility of defending the gospel. The Spirit can use evidence to convict men of the truth of the proclamation.[6]

While the argument is that utilizing any argument or defense limits or replaces the work of the Holy Spirit, the Scriptures say differently. The Apostle Peter states that when unbelievers or skeptics begin to question not only what we believe, we are to be prepared with an answer (apologia) and a defense of the faith. "Have no fear of them, nor be troubled, but in your hearts honor Christ the Lord as holy, always being prepared to make a defense to anyone who asks you for a reason for the hope that is in you. . ." (1 Pet 3:15). Notice how Peter reminds us that in preparing a reason for the hope we have, salvation in Christ from sin, death, and the devil, we "honor Christ." In no way do we supersede the work of the Holy Spirit with learning to defend the faith and then offering that evidence to unbelievers. Rather, we actually do the work of an evangelist (2 Tim 4:5) just as we are told.

While I stated that the focus in this book is the benefits of the Christian studying and then engaging in defending the faith, I think it is necessary that you see some of that proof. I've written extensively on this evidence in other books (*They Were Eyewitnesses* and *Creedal Apologetics*) but these will be touched on briefly here. Hopefully, it will whet your appetite to do more research and studying.

Easter is not primarily a comfort, but a challenge. Its message is either the supreme fact in history or else a gigantic hoax. Is the resurrection story just a nice message or beautiful story *or* is it full of spiritual meaning? Is it the supreme fact of history or not?

> If Christ is risen, nothing else matters.
> And if Christ is not risen, nothing else matters.[7]

When I first read that quote I was both floored and encouraged. It is said that Jaroslav made this statement on his deathbed. His confidence was ever in the risen Savior Jesus Christ. His hope rested in the fact that Jesus physically rose from the dead and he

---

6. Moreland, *Scaling the Secular City*, 14.
7. Pelikan, "If Christ Is Risen."

would as well. His educational mind looked at this as matter of fact and absolute truth. While I have several quotes that I keep track of, this one has taken a prominent place among them.

In our topsy-turvy world this is the hope of the Christian. In the craziness around us because Jesus rose from the grave we know our sins forgiven and our home is Heaven. Truly, the rest that goes on around us are just incidentals. The essential is that we have been forgiven of our sins and can call God Father through the work of the Holy Spirit by the written Word of God because Jesus lives.

On the opposite spectrum if Jesus did not rise from the dead, then as St. Paul tells us, we remain in our sins and should be pitied above everyone else in this world because we've fallen for a huge hoax. We are not forgiven and do not know God as our Father nor what will become of us after we die. We are truly miserable creatures, or accidents of the universe.

> And if Christ has not been raised, then our preaching is in vain and your faith is in vain. . . . We are even found to be misrepresenting God, because we testified about God that he raised Christ, whom he did not raise if it is true that the dead are not raised. For if the dead are not raised, not even Christ has been raised. . . . And if Christ has not been raised, your faith is futile and you are still in your sins. Then those also who have fallen asleep in Christ have perished. If in Christ we have hope in this life only, we are of all people most to be pitied. (1 Cor 15:14–19)

It is a great thing that Jesus did rise and our sins are forgiven and God has given us documented testimonial evidence in the shape and form of the Gospels and all of the Scriptures of this historical fact. If not, we would rely upon a myth or fable, a nice story. Since we have this evidence we can assure others that Christianity is not just rainbows and unicorns but facts and evidence that supports the facts. Just imagine if you had to rely upon feelings instead of the testimonial evidence to be assured of salvation. You would be as lost as the non-Christian coming to you for an answer for your faith. It is this testimonial evidence that I'll break down here to help you answer some questions.

First, this evidence is to assure you that we have a faith founded on fact and not feelings. It will be like the mortar between the bricks of the teachings of the Bible and will hold them together when the winds of uncertainty blow through your mind and heart during the storms of life. It will shore up your faith in a way that your personal testimony or experience never will. This is not about looking inside for assurance; subjective faith. This is about the objective truths God has gifted to His people.

Second, this evidence will give you answers to the many and varied questions you may be asked by friends, family, neighbors, coworkers, or in your social circle and social media. Here are the biblical proofs for the death, burial, and resurrection of Jesus Christ. This is where you can turn when they want proof because they are seriously seeking something real and true to hold on to in a world that seems upside down. This is what you can give them as an anchor in the storms and as the answer to their sinful condition.

Third, these brief evidences will also equip you to give a reason for the faith you have. These are reasonable answers to the Christian faith. These are simple facts. Put these evidences into your evangelism toolbox, learn about them and how to use them, and you will be equipped to both proclaim and defend the Christian faith when the time comes.

PROOFS OF THE RESURRECTION

Were the apostles liars or deluded simpletons? This is the key issue in Apologetics and when speaking with an unbeliever. They either think it a nice, wishful, hopeful story *or* they believe Jesus physically rose from the dead on the third day. No fence-sitting permitted. Either the apostles actually witnessed what happened on that Sunday after Jesus was crucified and buried or they have created the greatest hoax in history.

The problem with it being a hoax is that we have the Apostle Paul appealing, not only to the apostles and James the brother of

Jesus who didn't believe Jesus was messiah until He rose from the dead, but we have an appeal to over five hundred other people. St. Paul tells the Corinthian Christians that if they are struggling with the truth of the message that Jesus rose from the dead, go ask the five hundred eyewitnesses who were still alive and they will add their testimony to that of the apostles.

You have to admit, that's a pretty strong statement from the Apostle Paul and we can use it too. You see, documentary evidence is highly respected, valued, and relied upon in our courts of law. No one who knows something is a lie says to go check it out with one witness let alone five hundred eyewitnesses. Here, the apostle stakes his belief and his life on the fact that Jesus rose from the dead and showed Himself to over five hundred other people. How do we use that? We go to the documentary evidence; the Gospels and Acts. Here, written down from those who had personal knowledge of the events, is the evidence for Jesus' resurrection.

In the same way that an officer at the scene of an auto accident takes down and writes in his notes the accounts of those who were involved or were eyewitnesses to that event, so too the apostles wrote down what they saw and experienced themselves. The Gospels were written so that Christians would learn about the historical events that changed the world; Jesus' birth, life, death, burial, and resurrection. These were not fanciful tales to excite people. They were historical documents written down for the record that what they contain is the truth and we must believe them so that we might receive the forgiveness of our sins.

What is this evidence? While for the apostles and the five hundred eyewitnesses it happened in their own experience, we contemporary Christians need to call them to the stand when defending the faith. Who are they? Other than the five hundred, we have seven eyewitnesses who have given us their testimonies. These men saw Jesus risen and all but the Apostle John died excruciating deaths because of their testimony. Matthew, Mark, Luke, John, Paul, Peter, and James the brother of Jesus (who did not believe until after he saw Jesus risen from the dead) are who we turn to for proof. Their testimony is what we recall when defending the faith.

Christians need to review their testimonials over and over again so that when asked for proof we can present the facts. Becoming more and more versed in these statements in the Gospels and as recorded by St. Luke in Acts, we are better prepared to give an answer for our faith. However, knowing them builds us up and brings to us the assurance that what God tells us in the New Testament about Jesus is what in fact happened; Jesus died, was buried, and rose again for the forgiveness of our sins.

Here is a short summary of the documentary evidence, which we have contained in the New Testament, specifically the Four Gospels and the Book of Acts:

> Mark's Gospel: represents Peter's oral teaching (44 AD, possible Aramaic version in existence)
>
> Luke: Scholars admit his is a "minutely accurate historian. . ." (Anderson, *World's Religions*)
>
> Paul: Writes 1 Corinthians in 56 AD but gave believers this information orally in 49 AD and receive it from apostles before him in 40 AD (See Gal 1:18–19)

These first decade testimonies, the New Testament books, had no time to become a fable or faith tale as people living at the same time could refute the events. There are many other witnesses from those who hated the message of the apostles and evangelists, such as those in the Sanhedrin, who could have refuted the events as well but didn't. Paul, in his letter to the Corinthians, states that if they doubted the resurrection there were over five hundred eyewitnesses, many still alive, whom they would be able to verify the message with. If Paul knew the resurrection to be a lie, why would he recommend they seek out and ask the other eyewitnesses? The men and women who personally experienced and saw Jesus risen from the death lived out the highest moral and ethical teachings in the world. They were men and women of whom this world was not worthy to have. They were honest, caring, loving, gracious, and noble. Though each would probably tell you they were sinners saved by grace. If we were to believe they lied it would be absolutely contradictory to their teachings.

The resurrection of Jesus changed cowards into heroes and brave men and women who often died the martyr's death. They faced the mouths of beasts in the arenas around the Roman Empire. They were crucified, torched, and burned to death or executed in various ways all because they testified that Jesus is Lord and the One who rose from the dead conquering sin, death, and the grave. They boldly proclaimed that Jesus forgives sins and is Lord of all in front of proconsuls, courts, and even caesars all because they were the eyewitnesses of these events. Those men and women who cowered in the upper room before the resurrection now boldly gave their lives to the executioner's blade because they knew it to be true.

Under the threat of agonizing deaths they continued to testify to the events and facts that Jesus died, was buried, and rose from the dead for the forgiveness of sins. They did not value their lives but the life of the resurrected One who had redeemed them. Under this type of stress, if what they were testifying to were a lie, one of the twelve or the five hundred eyewitnesses, or Luke or Paul, would have yielded and exclaimed it a lie. However, not one stated it was a hoax; instead, with unyielding trust in the fact of Jesus' resurrection, entered that which He had prepared for them: Heaven. This should bolster your own faith when challenged and encourage you to realize that we have the facts on our side. As Christians we also may face fierce objections to our faith someday. The fact that they did and never faltered should strengthen and buttress your faith in the risen Savior, Jesus Christ our Lord.

Going against the cultural norms of the day, God used women as the first eyewitnesses. In Roman and Jewish society their testimony was not held in high esteem or even respected. Yet, these who first went to the tomb, and Mary who spoke to Jesus after His resurrection, are the ones God chose to tell the men, the disciples who were hiding in fear. The New Testament, in this instance, crushes the gender roles of that day. In today's society this wouldn't seem so important, but two thousand years ago this was extraordinary: women as key witnesses. No writer of books would do this. No forger or liar, trying to convince others of his made up story, would employ women as the first eyewitnesses. It just would not be done. This, alone, would negate the entire account. People would dispute it on its face. Yet, this is still who God used to tell the disciples/apostles that Jesus was risen from the dead and alive forevermore.

Now add to using women as the first eyewitness that it is Mary Magdalene and you have to wonder what forger would use her? Why wouldn't he use a respected person like John, who had an in with the courts in Jerusalem? Or Nathanael, Matthew, James, or even Peter? This goes directly against the culture and norm for the day two thousand years ago.

Then we have the accounts of various people heading to the tomb. These accounts are just too detailed to be an orchestrated lie. You see, if you lie, and it is a group lie, you've got to make it simple to remember. So, the less details the better. But not the New Testament accounts. They are too extremely detailed and from various perspectives to be made up. From the various Gospel accounts of that first day we read of Mary confusing Jesus for a gardener, Peter and John running to the tomb, of the grave clothes with the face cloth all folded up neatly separated from the rest of the bands, the discussions between the women and men, the later account of the men who were heading to Emmaus who met the risen Jesus on the journey, and the accounts of the soldiers to the Jewish leaders. It is all just too detailed to be a corroborative hoax and lie. There are just too many details to remember for it to be a lie and therefore, must be the truth.

There are various reasons people give for not believing. These are either that the disciples stole the body (Matt 28:11–15) or the authorities removed the body. Why? Then the disciples would say He was risen. That was the reason for the guards to begin with. Why would the authorities then admit fishermen and tax collectors overpowered Roman guards and stole the body of Jesus? In fact, the detail was so secured that if that had happened the Roman soldiers would have been executed for failing their duty. Also, if the authorities did remove the bodies, then when rumors of His resurrection began to filter in through town and the country, why not simply present the body as proof against it?

Ever wonder why it takes seven more weeks for the disciples to proclaim the resurrection? Why a delay? Why, if this is their scenario, does it take seven weeks more for the disciples to proclaim the risen Savior? If they made it up, they would declare it immediately. However, they don't. They continue to hide and then even go back to work (fishing). They do nothing about this news until the day of Pentecost when they receive the power to be witnesses to this historic event.

The Swoon Theory was invented by Venturini at the end of the eighth century and holds that Jesus swooned on the cross, which was caused by the agony of crucifixion and loss of blood but the cool restfulness of the tomb revived Him. Are we to believe that after three days in a dark damp tomb with no food or medical care, that Jesus revives himself? Are we to believe that Jesus recovered so completely from mortal wounds that He pushes the stone away from inside and takes over the Roman guards? Are we to believe that He did this while wrapped in a cocoon of spice-laden (seventy pounds or more) grave cloths? Are we, then, to believe He walked back to Jerusalem, in grave clothes and on feet that had been nailed to wood three days before? Are we to believe that this is the "conqueror" of death and the grave? Limping to Jerusalem, needing sustenance and medical attention?

It could be a mass illusion or hallucination. This is impossible. No two people can experience the same exact hallucination. The mind is highly individual as is the subconscious and mind.

The Christian church is born. From the beginning the Christian church began to meet on the first day of the week. Keep in mind, each of the first Christians were Jewish and to worship on any day other than the Sabbath (last day of the week) would be unthinkable. Yet, these men and women gather together on the first day of the week. Why? Jesus rose on the first day of the week and they were commemorating it. They changed the day of worship

Experience or Evidence?

from Saturday to Sunday in commemoration of the resurrection of Jesus Christ.

This sad little company of defeated cowards, hiding in a house in Jerusalem, fearing they're next for the cross, becomes a band of irresistible missionaries who turned the world upside down and whom no opposition could deter. These evangelists and apostles, who feared death before the resurrection, now face death head on with absolute assurance that because Jesus lives they will also. These eyewitnesses offer us their testimonials so that we too will be assured that "the third day He rose again from the dead . . . sits at the right hand of God . . . from thence He will come to judge the living and the dead."[8]

---

8. Commission on Worship of the Lutheran Church—Missouri Synod, *Lutheran Service Book*, 159.

3

Educated & Equipped

THE BIBLE COMMANDS THAT WE GIVE a reasoned defense of the faith in 1 Pet 3:15. Peter also makes it clear this is to be done by first setting apart Christ as Lord in your heart and to do this with gentleness and respect. This is not about just getting a few bits and pieces of information but of studying the Scriptures, the great creeds of Christianity and the confessions of our faith. Often times, you will find the answer to those who ask in the Bible and then succinctly stated by the early church or the Reformers. So, theologically speaking, we should agree with the phrase, why reinvent the wheel? Sometimes, though, we just need to put it into our own language and this can only be done successfully if you've studied.

Now, I know, I've said this is not a lesson book on Apologetics but rather, a book to encourage you to actually engage in Apologetics, the defending of the Christian faith. Yet, in any and every vocation we have in life, we look either to mentors or books to teach us. If you are a doctor, you studied the textbooks but then went through residency where a seasoned physician helped guide you. If you are a mom, you often go to the older women at church or in your neighborhood and ask for advice. The same with Apologetics. We first go to the source, the Scriptures, then the mentors, the creeds and confessions, and then to our contemporaries. Why? Because they've been in the apologetical ditch and know the benefits and practicalities of defending the faith.

Scripture is clear that we are to have a ready defense. Christians must obey the Scriptures. Therefore, if you don't know what you believe and cannot defend the faith, then you are disobeying God's Word. I know there are many excuses Christians try to bring up for not doing Apologetics but none of them can be proven from the Scripture. Some Christians have said to me, "I don't know enough about the Bible. . ." or "I don't want to get into a theological debate. . ." or "I'm not a pastor or professor. . ." Every one of them is an excuse to disobey the Word of God.

The Apostle Peter was writing to people in the pew. He wasn't just writing to other apostles or elders or deacons. St. Peter wrote to the farmer, fishermen, seamen, carpenters, masons, moms, and dads whether young or old. In the broader sense, Peter wrote to you and me. He wrote to the everyday Christian that they need to have a reason ready for why they believe in the resurrection of Jesus. Peter did not tell the Christians of his day, or ours for that matter, if they ask why you believe what you believe to tell them to talk to your pastor. He did not tell them to avoid theological discussions. In fact, there is an urgency to Peter's imperative: a ready defense.

This ready defense does not mean you pre-plan your conversation. It does mean that you plan for conversations. Christians should be ready to engage the culture and the people around them with the truth of the Gospel. How else will they be saved unless you tell them? (cf. Rom 10). Most people who are not Christians (sadly some who claim to be Christians) will not step foot in a church. It is one of your vocations (we wear many vocational hats) to have an answer for their inquiries.

How, though, does this effect you? If you study and read, your own faith will be strengthened. Now, while God uses the Means of Grace to strengthen our faith, this is not what I'm saying. When you know the evidences for the Christian faith, you realize that we have a reasonable faith and not the pie in the sky ideas of other religions. Our faith is based on fact. This truth then strengthens our understanding of the faith. When we understand it better, we then communicate it better.

For Christians, the study of God's Word is essential. We need to know the *what* of our belief. That is what is called doctrine. The study of doctrine is theology or study of God (theo = God; logos = Word). When we study God's Word, the truth sets into our hearts and minds. God has not called us to a mindless faith. We've been called to know God and His Gospel. How do we do that? We learn through the preaching and hearing of the Word each week and through the study and reading of it daily. Leave off of reading and studying and soon enough you either weaken your faith or you become uninformed and wander away. Christians need to study God's Word.

How should we study? Does it need to be formal education? As we read God's Word daily and look into our confessions, we learn. For some, they may want to take a formal class in Apologetics (check out the weekly #ApologeticsTogether course offered at Lutherangirl.org) but for many it will be informal.

At the beginning of this book I quoted Jude 20: "But you, beloved, building yourselves up in your most holy faith." Scripture tells us that when we study and then contend for the faith it helps to build us up in our faith. That's a remarkable result. Perhaps we should think of it as building confidence in the faith. Confidence builds in us that what we believe is factual and true. Confidence in the Christian faith encourages us to tell others these truths. When you know the proofs for the Christian faith you will be encouraged to both proclaim and defend in a way that honors the name of Christ and challenges to unbeliever to examine and see for themselves that Jesus died, was buried, and rose again for the forgiveness of our sins.

When I first took Apologetics, I thought I would learn how to argue and debate. Nothing could be further from the truth. Dr. Montgomery took us through the evidences of the Scriptures to teach us that our faith has a sure and solid foundation. He brought us through the testimonies of the apostles and evangelists and taught us how to take note of the key points and share them with others. It was emphasized that Apologetics was not an optional skill for believers and was to be a tool used in evangelism.

While critical thinking skills were learned and honed, first and foremost we were taught to listen. Listen carefully to their questions. Listen to what they really want to hear because often their initial question is covering up what they really want to know. When we think more critically we can offer the unbeliever solid reasons for them to believe. When we think critically we can pull away the hurdles, one by one, which keep them from true faith in Christ. When we think critically we have honed our skills at keeping on point and focusing on what matters; Jesus died, was buried, and rose again for the forgiveness of their sins.

Apologetics is not about debate. It is simply a tool you can learn to help you when presenting the Gospel message. Since it is not about debating, that tends to take the wall of fear down that many have about Apologetics. Since it is about proclaiming the Gospel, perhaps it will remind you that the most important message you can bring to an unbeliever is the life-giving Gospel message that Jesus rose again so that we might be forgiven.

When we Christians engage in Apologetics it builds up our confidence and faith in the One who conquered death, Hell, and the grave. It strengthens us inwardly, building us up in the knowledge of truth. Engaging in Apologetics also equips us as it teaches us the skills of defending the faith and also giving us knowledge about the truthfulness and uniqueness of the Christian faith. No other religion, and I teach world religions, has the objective evidence that Christianity does. Christianity is not based on personal testimonies, spiritual experiences, or anything subjective. Doubt can arise from subjective proofs. However, Christianity is unique in that its main teaching, the life, death, and resurrection of Jesus, is founded on facts.

Nineteenth-century philosopher John Stuart Mill said,

> He who knows only his own side of the case knows little of that. His reasons may be good, and no one may have been able to refute them. But if he is equally unable to

> refute the reasons on the opposite side, if he does not so much as know what they are, he has no ground for preferring either opinion.[1]

When I studied Apologetics I began to learn about other world views. I grew up in a Christian home and knew almost nothing of other religions or viewpoints. Apologetics educated me on the religions of the world as well as agnosticism, humanism, and atheism. Apologetics then equipped me, through educating me, to enter conversations with those of different religions/beliefs in a more confident manner. Knowing what they believed, in comparison to Christianity, I now had the tools to begin showing them where their religion faltered and where Christianity stood above all other belief systems. Apologetics took the fear out of the reasons why I believe and, honestly, out of sharing those reasons. I did not have to argue; instead, I could calmly and reasonably bring to them the unique truth of Christianity. Debate-styled discussions became friendly conversations. In Apologetics, I learned I didn't have to argue but instead I was providing proofs for Christianity in a gentle and peaceful manner.

This led to another result for me, personally, as a Christian: I was equipped. I was better equipped to respond to their questions. I was better equipped to bring them the Gospel. I was better equipped to answer for my own faith and reasons why I personally believe the Good News of the resurrection of Jesus. This made me breathe easier. That I knew there were reasons behind Christianity meant I could better share the faith with others. Apologetics equipped me to proclaim the faith, not just defend it.

Knowing the reasons to believe did not result in pride. In fact, the result was less arguing and more listening. It resulted in humbling me because I knew our great God had given such wonderful gifts through the testimonial and documentary evidence provided in the Scriptures.

Let me digress here with some of that documented evidence from an article I wrote on my blog:

1. Anderson, "Reasons to Study Apologetics."

When one compares the Gospels to other ancient documents with regard to their bibliography it becomes evident that we have an overabundance of support for the validity and accuracy as well as the reliability of the Gospel accounts. In the well-regarded book by Josh McDowell entitled *The New Evidence that Demands a Verdict*, the following chart is given:

Author	When Written	Earliest Copy	Time Span	No. of Copies
Homer (Iliad)	900 BC	400 BC	500 years	643
Caesar (The Gallic Wars)	100 - 44 BC	900 AD	1,000 years	10
Plato (Tetralogies)	427 - 347 BC	900 AD	1,200 years	7
Aristotle	384 - 322 BC	1,100 AD	1,400 years	49
Herodotus (History)	480 - 425 BC	900 AD	1,300 years	8
Euripedes	480 - 406 BC	1,100 AD	1,500 years	9
New Testament	50 - 90 A.D.	130 AD (possibly now 40-70AD with Magdalene Manuscript)	30 years	24,000

This chart was adapted from charts in *The New Evidence that Demands a Verdict*, by Josh McDowell, 1999, page 38.[1]

The importance of the overwhelming number of manuscript copies cannot be overstated. If the same tests for bibliography that are used for other ancient manuscripts are then applied to the Gospel and New Testament texts, the Gospels are proven beyond a shadow of a doubt to be authentic and reliable. Sir Frederic G. Kenyon states:

> Besides number, the manuscripts of the New Testament differ from those of the classical authors. . . . In no other case is the interval of time between the composition of the book and the date of the earliest extant manuscripts so short as in that of the New Testament. . . . The interval then between the dates of the original composition and the earliest extant evidence becomes so small as to be in fact negligible, and the last foundation for any doubt that the Scriptures have come down to us substantially as they were written has now been removed.[2]

Another authority on the Scriptures is F. F. Bruce and he writes: "There is no body of ancient literature in the world which

2. Kenyon, *Bible and Archaeology*, 89.

enjoys such a wealth of good textual attestation as the New Testament."[3] In fact, the quotations from the New Testament documents are so numerous and widespread that if we were to lose the manuscripts, the New Testament writings could be reproduced by the writings of the apostolic fathers alone. When one compares the quotes from the early fathers with the writings from the manuscripts it becomes evident that what has come down to us as the inspired Word of God has been maintained in its original form; there is no redaction or editing that can be verified but instead the integrity of the original words are maintained.

Sir David Dalrymple stated that he had "found the entire New Testament except eleven verses"[4] in the writings of the early church fathers. From the writings and materials that Dean Brugon compiled we have over 85,000 quotations from the New Testament written by the patristic fathers.[5] Based upon the above evidence from bibliographical, internal, and external tests, which is really barely scratching the surface of all the evidence we do have, one can conclude that the New Testament is amply proven to be valid and accurate.

With regards to the internal test one must, as Prof. John Warwick Montgomery states, still follow Aristotle's dictum that "the benefit of the doubt is to be given to the document itself, not arrogated by the critic to himself."[6] Paul, in writing to the Corinthians, expresses to them that his own office of apostle was validated before them through signs, wonders, and miracles (cf. 2 Cor 12:12). This would have been ludicrous on the part of Paul if he wasn't speaking the truth. This second letter to the Corinthians was written to those whom he had ministered personally and could have easily been refuted by the Corinthians themselves if Paul had been lying.

When Paul stood before King Agrippa and gave testimony to the validity of the Christian faith he expressed that all these

---

3. Bruce, *Books and the Parchments*, 178.
4. Torrey, *Our Bible*, 35.
5. McDowell, *New Evidence*, 132.
6. Warwick, *Faith Founded on Fact*, 129.

things, the life of Jesus, the crucifixion, death, and burial, and even the resurrection were not "done in a corner" (Acts 26:26). Once again, if the Apostle had been lying surely King Agrippa would have stated that at Paul's trial. But King Agrippa doesn't deny the testimony of Paul but is nearly persuaded by it. These few instances show that the internal test for integrity within the New Testament documents remains intact and is passed.

When the New Testament is brought to the bar of the external test for accuracy, faithfulness, and integrity one is forced to face an abundance of evidence once again. The question to be answered by the external test is whether or not other historical materials confirm or deny the internal testimony provided by the documents themselves. With regard to the integrity of the New Testament documents and manuscripts, the weight of evidence is on the side of the validity of these documents. One can compare the patristic citations of Scripture as witnesses both to the compilation of documents that have come down to us as the inspired Word of God as well as the very words themselves.

The quotations from the New Testament documents are so numerous and widespread that if we were to lose the manuscripts, the New Testament writings could be reproduced by the writings of the apostolic fathers alone. When one compares the quotes from the early fathers with the writings from the manuscripts it becomes evident that what has come down to us as the inspired Word of God has been maintained in its original form; there is no redaction or editing that can be verified, but instead the integrity of the original words are maintained. Sir David Dalrymple stated that he had "found the entire New Testament except eleven verses"[7] in the writings of the early church fathers. From the writings and materials that Dean Brugon compiled, we have over 85,000 quotations from the New Testament written by the patristic fathers.[8]

Based upon the above evidence from bibliographical, internal, and external tests, which is really barely scratching the surface

---

7. Torrey, *Our Bible*, 35.
8. McDowell, *New Evidence*, 78.

of all the evidence we do have, one can conclude that the New Testament is amply proven to be valid and accurate.

When Christians understand the amount of proof God has given His people for the truthfulness of the life, death, burial, and resurrection of Jesus they no longer need to argue. Instead, we can confidently offer the inquiring unbeliever these evidences and then proclaim to them the One who is "the way, the truth, and the life" (John 14:6) through whom they may receive life eternal. By learning and studying Apologetics we are educated to know what we believe and why and then equipped to go out and proclaim the glorious Gospel of Jesus Christ and the forgiveness of sins.

Of course, none of us have the answers to every question the inquirer may bring up but that should not dissuade us but rather push us on to study more. When challenged, our response should become, "let me get back to you on that," continuing the conversation in the future. Learning Apologetics does this and more for the believer and it is my desire that you begin the journey so that God may use you, fully equipped, with a ready defense to proclaim the Good News to one more person before He calls you home to Himself.

4

Encouraged & Excited

WHEN CHRISTIANS BEGIN TO learn Apologetics and all the reasons and evidence behind our faith we become excited and are greatly encouraged. Though evangelicalism has laid the burden of proof upon personal experience and testimonies, God has given us the reasons for believing in His promises. This is such an encouragement to the Christian. We have a thinking faith. We have a reasonable faith. We have an objective faith. We have the one true faith.

Knowing the evidences, even the few presented in the previous chapters, encourages us so that we can answer when they ask why we believe. Examining the evidence for ourselves strengthens our faith. When we read of the testimonies of the evangelists and Gospel writers, we too can say, as Luther wrote in his Small Catechism: This is most certainly true.

When we lean on our own experiences the one asking us about Christianity can respond, "Well, that's just your own experience/feelings/belief." This can lead us to despair because how do you prove the subjective. You cannot. Evidence must be objective to be provable. Your salvation experience, whether it was baptized as an infant or adult convert, whether you signed some decision card or walked down some aisle, is not the point of Apologetics or evangelism. You cannot prove that what you personally experienced within is true. That excitement you feel recalling your adult conversion, those butterflies in the stomach, may just be something you ate that is disagreeable to your system. Rejoice! God has not left us without a witness, even creation (Acts 14:17) but more so, the apostles and evangelists in the whole of the New Testament.

When I first learned the evidences and documentary testimonies, I was greatly encouraged to learn more. I was also encouraged to share with others what I was learning. Some whom I shared with argued with me that the proof was in what I experienced. Now, granted, my adult conversion was dramatic in some of the immediate changes to my lifestyle but it was still subjective. Perhaps I had simply realized I should lead a moral life and be kinder. Or perhaps I had gotten hold of some self-improvement text and was simply applying the principles to my life. You see, subjective experience can be rejected. My own boss, at the time, thought I'd had a mental breakdown and offered his own therapist to evaluate me. I didn't know enough at the time to show him the documentary evidence and so, after our discussion in which my whole proof was subjective, he left saying to me, "you almost persuaded me. . ." Oh how miserable I felt when I left his office. I had given him my personal testimony of the experience and it proved nothing to him.

One other issue with sharing our personal testimony is that some may have a quiet one like Nathanael in the Gospel of John while others may have dramatic ones like Peter. Most people want the dramatic and if their own conversion testimony isn't well they may feel dejected or somehow less of a Christian. So, when we leave our personal testimony to present the biblical evidences, then no one is comparing themselves to another person. Instead, they are looking at the objective evidence, the eyewitness testimonies, and either they are brought to faith or they reject it.

The encouragement that the study of Apologetics brings is that you can present the evidence and it does speak for itself. The evidence is none less than the Word of God, the Gospel of salvation. This is what God promises will be the power of salvation. The Apostle Paul, in Romams 10, reminds us that what the unbeliever needs to hear is the gospel, the death, burial, and resurrection of Jesus, according to the Scriptures. God uses the means of preaching and proclaiming this Good News to gift the unbeliever with saving faith. He does the work through you as you present the reasons to believe. That is encouraging.

This encouragement then has another interesting result: excitement. Many fear answering questions about our faith because we are stuck in our experience instead of knowing how to present the reasons for Christianity. Many Christians feel they don't know enough to answer so they tell the person, "Go speak to my pastor." Too many unbelievers just won't do that and so they walk away not knowing the real reasons you believe. However, when you know the reasons to believe, the solid evidences that God's Word has laid out, you gain excitement to tell the unbeliever. You get excited to evangelize. When you understand the reasons to reason with them you want to bring those evidences to the conversation.

Excitement to proclaim and share the Good News almost naturally comes out of the encouragements you have received from learning Apologetic tools. You will not have all the answers but you have the one who is the answer to their ultimate question: Where will I go when I die?

It is a key component of Apologetics to know and understand the reasons to reason with your unbelieving friend. Your excitement will come when proclaiming the objective truth to them results in a gospel proclamation and the Holy Spirit gifts them true faith in Jesus Christ. Imagine, if you will, this scenario:

> Your doorbell rings and as you open the door you find two very nice young adults standing there offering you material to read. You take it graciously and begin to scan and see that they are here at your home to introduce you to their religion. You read the material and begin to ask them this very important question, "How do you know your religion is the true one?"
>
> Their typical response is this, "We know it's true because we can feel it in our heart."

You respond, "That's fascinating because I too believe that my religion is true because I can feel it in my heart."

You are now at a standoff. Which subjective testimony is true? Which one is the Truth?

Now, let's change that since you've begun studying Apologetics:

Your doorbell rings and as you open the door you find two very nice young adults standing there offering you material to read. You take it graciously and begin to scan and see that they are here at your home to introduce you to their religion. You read the material and begin to ask them this very important question, "How do you know your religion is the true one?"

Their typical response is this, "We know it's true because we can feel it in our heart."

You respond, "That is wonderful. I too believe Christianity to be true, but it is based on objective evidence and not my subjective feelings. You see, sometimes my emotions get the best of me and I don't quite feel it. However, because there is objective evidence, eyewitness testimonies, and documentary evidence, I know it is true. Come, let's sit down and talk about this evidence so that you too may know the true religion."

You are no longer at a standoff except for the truth God's Word has given us as evidences for the Christian faith. Oh, they may walk away but they no longer have the excuse that they've never heard the real gospel.

As shared with me by someone who has taken my Apologetics courses, they no longer feel unequipped to discuss Christianity. Now they no longer fear the questions and are excited about answering them. Oh, you won't have all the answers right up front, and you will need to study more, but you will have all that you need to point to Jesus Christ who died, was buried, and rose again according to the Scriptures. You will be able to share the eyewitness testimonies from the New Testament with them. You will be able to reason with them and proclaim that Jesus died and rose again for the forgiveness of our sins.

An unforeseen benefit of studying Apologetics is that it also helps us to help our Christian friends who may be in a church that does not teach the whole counsel of God. They may be in a church that proclaims error at best and heresy at worst. Imagine being able to reason with them and share the truth in a way that helps them see the errors they are in. You see, error has always tried to wedge its way between the foundation stones of Christianity in order to bring about its fall. So, learning about the proofs of the faith, the objective truth we have, is simply a way to help bring them back, as Paul said to Jude, to our most holy faith (Jude 20).

Apologetics builds up our faith, encourages us to recognize the reasons to believe, and excites us to share the truth to those both outside and inside the church. While we contend for the faith with those espousing error we also must contend with those who do not yet believe. As we are encouraged in the faith we begin to confidently, albeit I'm sure with pounding hearts and knocking knees, present the Gospel to all whom God sends our way.

When Christians study Apologetics, we are taught sound doctrine and kept more firmly in the truth. Then, we are better equipped to share these truths with others presenting the Gospel with the objective evidence. Whether they believe or not is not up to how strong or sound your arguments. We must always remember that our vocation is to proclaim, have a reason for why we believe, and present it honestly, with gentleness, humility, and meekness. We aren't here to win arguments or debates. Instead, with our own knowledge of the Christian faith shored up through the skills learned in Apologetics, we leave the converting to God's Holy Spirit. He will take what has been presented and use that to bring them to true faith.

The study of Apologetics is the way to respond to the unbeliever's questions by simply saying, "These are the reasons I believe. . ." But, let me remind you that you may have understood the Christian faith better because someone explained the reasons it is the one true religion using Apologetics, but ultimately, Apologetics is simply a tool of evangelism and it is God who gives anyone true faith. Never rely upon the strength, eloquence, soundness, or determination in your reasons to believe but upon God's Holy Spirit to convince, convict, and convert.

5

Endurance

THIS WILL BE A short chapter focused upon one result of the Christian personally studying Apologetics.

No one knows what will happen in their generation. Will Christians be permitted to live their lives in quietness and peace? Or, will persecution come?

What does the study of Apologetics have to do with endurance? It is simply one tool God has given us to shore up our own faith when tested. When the Apostles were challenged regarding the reasons they believed that Jesus conquered sin, death, and the grave, they did not say, "I know Jesus lives because He lives in my heart." As nice a hymn as that is, it is completely focused on the wrong reasons. Your feelings will falter. Your faith will be tested. What are you basing it upon? The fleeting feelings and emotional experiences you testify about? No. But the absolute truth of God's Word, the testimonies we have from the Scriptures, that is what will stand the test.

When Peter was telling the Christians in his letter to have an answer ready, he was writing to those who had been thrown out of their homes because of their faith. He was encouraging those under persecution to be ready to answer those who were dead set against the message of the crucified and risen One, Jesus. He was reminding them that they have reasons to believe and it is not just all in their heart.

In the same way, Jude reminds us that "in the last time there will be scoffers, following their own ungodly passions . . . but you, beloved, building yourselves up in your most holy faith and praying in the Holy Spirit keep yourselves in the love of God, waiting for the mercy of our Lord Jesus Christ that leads to eternal life" (Jude 17–21). Not only does Apologetics offer the unbeliever reasons to believe but it builds up the Christian in their faith.

Scripture is filled with those who endured to the end. Church history is laced with the testimonies and martyrdom of those who endured to the end. Their stalwart faithfulness should serve to encourage Christians in each and every generation to endure to the end. Jesus promises us the crown of life if we but endure to the end.

As I was reading the text from the Revelation of John (2:10b), "Be faithful unto death, and I will give you the crown of life," I began to go back to the beginning of chapter two. There was an interesting thing about nearly all of the seven churches that John writes to: they are each enduring in some fashion, even the churches that are being a bit scolded to straighten up.

To the church in Ephesus, Jesus says, "I know your works, your toil and your patient endurance, and how you cannot bear with those who are evil, but have tested those who call themselves apostles and are not, and found them to be false. I know you are enduring patiently and bearing up for my name's sake, and you have not grown weary" (Rev 2:2–3). A closer look teaches us that the Ephesians do not permit false teachers to remain. Even then, just as it is now, there are those who call themselves apostles and are not. In my book *A Modern Ninety-Five* I go through the requirements of an apostle and these evidently do not meet that requirement.

Here is what I wrote:

> Therefore, if by the term "apostle" we mean "one who is sent on a mission," then that is still a functioning office. If by the term we mean one who has biblical authority, has seen the Risen Christ personally, has infallibility

in preaching, has a direct call from God, and performs signs and wonders on demand, then this is the criteria by which we challenge the claimant to prove by the written Word of God that his or her authority is from above. . . . Peter in his discourse in the upper room gives the criteria for apostleship which we read in Acts 1:21–22. So one of the men who have accompanied us during all the time that the Lord Jesus went in and out among us, beginning from the baptism of John until the day when he was taken up from us—one of these men must become with us a witness to his resurrection (Acts 1:21–22). The position of the apostles was unique to them and to Paul—all directly chosen by Christ Jesus with no hint of succession. In the New Testament, the apostles appointed not apostles but rather elders and deacons.[1]

It never ceases to amaze me how accurate the Scriptures are. The Preacher wrote:

> What has been is what will be,
>   and what has been done is what will be done,
>   and there is nothing new under the sun. (Eccl 1:10 ESV)

In the Book of Revelation we find Christ telling John how false apostles had already arisen, even while the Apostle John was alive, and in today's churches many claim to be apostles. However, as we read in Acts, the biblical qualifications for holding that office, we learn that it is impossible to be an apostle because no one living today, or since the death of the last apostle (John), saw the risen Christ personally. Yet, here we are and many claim this office. The question remains, then, do you, Christian, find them to be false as the church in Ephesus did? Or, are you accepting them and blindly following them instead of God's Word.

You see, part of enduring to the end is being able to discern the true from the false. The accolade given to the church in Ephesus was that part of their "enduring patiently" was testing those who claimed to be apostles by what they taught and said. You see,

---

1. Almodovar, *Modern Ninety-Five*, location 206 of 2915.

Apologetics also works within the church. You no longer endure their false claims or teachings but hold fast to the true teachings of the Bible.

By you, the Christian, reading the Scriptures prayerfully, heeding all that it says, and believing it to be the true Word of God, you can test those who come to you with some new teaching. Testing what they say, exactly like the Bereans did when the Apostle Paul taught them (Acts 17:11) to "examine the Scriptures daily to see if these things (what Paul was preaching) were so," is what Christians are called to do. How we do that is through studying the Word, learning from church history, and believing the ecumenical creeds (Apostles', Nicaean, and Athanasian) and confessions, prayerfully considering and meditating upon them. Christians learn to endure through the attacks by believing that which is truth. As Jesus said in His prayer, "Thy Word is Truth" (John 17:17).

The encouragement to the church in Ephesus was also, "I know you are enduring patiently and bearing up for my name's sake, and you have not grown weary" (Rev 2:3). While they certainly had some things wrong, this statement should be that of every believer. When we are persecuted for our faith we should continue to bear up the name of Jesus Christ as the One who died, was buried, and rose again according to the Scriptures. We are called Christians, little christs (Acts 11:26), precisely because His name was placed upon us at our baptism. We believe in Him because He died and shed His blood for the forgiveness of our sins. We are never to be ashamed of this truth and through Apologetics we have learned the reasons behind our faith. We have found that these reasons are very, well, reasonable. We have learned that because He was raised from the dead, we too were raised to newness of life (Rom 6:4) and that when this earthly tent is shed, we will be with Him. This is the faith that the church in Ephesus remained steadfast upon and endured with great patience.

The Apostle Paul's reminder to the church in Corinth was similar when he writes, "When reviled, we bless; when persecuted, we endure" (1 Cor 4:12). Then to the Romans he wrote, "Who shall

ENDURANCE

separate us from the love of Christ? Shall tribulation, or distress, or persecution, or famine, or nakedness, or danger, or sword?" (Rom 8:35). "Indeed, all who desire to live a godly life in Christ Jesus will be persecuted" (2 Tim 3:12). You see, in every age the church has been persecuted and yet still stands. Those who endure to the end, through the trials and persecutions, will receive that crown of life that is promised in Revelation (Rev 2:10b).

To my own amazement, I began to notice that even though Jesus had to rebuke and correct some things in the various churches that John is to write to, there are also encouragements and each one is quite similar: they do not deny the risen Christ. To the church in Pergamum, He says, "Yet, you hold fast my name and you did not deny my faith even in the days of Antipas my faithful witness" (Rev 2:13). The Pergamum Christians refused to reject the name of Jesus by whom comes the forgiveness of sins. We know from the Apostle Peter's sermons that "there is one name given under Heaven whereby men can be saved" (ff. Acts 2:21, 38; 4:12; 10:43; 22:16). Since we have studied Apologetics, the reasons to believe (though certainly saving faith is a gift of God not based upon human argument), we have been strengthened in the inner man to endure to the end, God willing. It is His name we confess and profess. It is who He is, what He has done, that we proclaim, and it is His resurrection that we defend against all antagonists.

To Thyatira's church Jesus says, "I know your works, your love and faith and service and patient endurance" (Rev 2:19). Once again, Jesus encourages them by saying, "I know . . ." They are enduring with patience in a time of severe persecution. Many are martyred for the Christian faith and they have remained steadfast in their confession of faith, proclaiming the name of Christ above the false gods of the time. They believed Jesus rose again through the promise given at their baptism; they would rise again too. In fact, Paul taught them that they were raised at the time of their baptism with water and the Word.

In the *Treasury of Daily Prayer*, the writing for February 10 by Hermann Sasse says,

> God views us in baptism as people who have already died and been raised, put to death with His beloved Son on Golgotha and raised from the dead on Easter morning. Thus He already views us as such who already believe, the poorest, weakest little child which we bring to Holy Baptism.[2]

In the font of baptism they were granted saving faith and our great God placed His own name upon them and us. This is the name we declare to those who do not yet know Him. This is whose name we defend as we engage in Apologetics. Apologetics teaches us the reasons to reason and equips, educates, and encourages us to endure to the end.

To Sardis, Jesus reminds them that only the "one who conquers will be clothed thus in white garments, and I will never blot his name out of the book of Life" (Rev 3:5). Here we see from a different angle the effects of endurance. Sardis Christians are faltering. They have forgotten the one that bought them. They were not remaining faithful. They were failing to endure to the end. So, Jesus reminds and encourages them to remember the reasons to believe and endure and the reward awaiting those who stand to the end. Contemporary Christians need this encouragement just as much as the Christians in Sardis. We will not be found naked in the end if we endure but clothed with the righteous robes of Jesus Christ.

To the church in Philadelphia, Jesus is quite plainly speaking that they "have not denied my name" (Rev 2:8). Throughout their persecution they remained steadfast. In fact, Jesus says, "Because you have kept my word about patient endurance, I will keep you from the hour of trial." Yet, they are to "hold fast"(Rev 3:10) and not waver. They are to remain faithful to the end. We too, just like the believers in Philadelphia, are to patiently endure to the end no matter what comes our way. Knowing what you believe and why you believe it aides your endurance and strengthens your faith through the Means of Grace in the proclaimed Word of God, which teaches us to never deny His name.

2. *Treasury of Daily Prayer*, 1197.

Endurance

Even to the Laodicean church, Jesus exhorts them to endure when He says, "The one who conquers, I will grant him to sit with me on my throne, as I also conquered and sit down with my Father on His throne" (Rev 3:21) Wow! That is some promise! If we endure, if we conquer the fears and sins within, through the Means of Grace of course, we will sit with Jesus on the throne.

Jesus says that just as He endured, we too must endure. The writer to Hebrews says it this way:

> ... and let us run with endurance the race that is set before us, looking to Jesus, the founder and perfecter of our faith, who for the joy that was set before him endured the cross, despising the shame, and is seated at the right hand of the throne of God. Consider him (Jesus) who endured from sinners such hostility against himself, so that you may not grow weary or fainthearted. (Heb 12:1b-3)

This passage comes right after the chapter on the saints of old who endured to the end and did not see the fulfilment of the prophecies and promises concerning Jesus Christ for He had not yet come. To Christians, on the other side of the death, burial, and resurrection of Jesus, we too are to endure to the end.

The Christian life is an endurance race. It is a marathon and not a sprint. It is long, hard, tiresome, and dangerous. Yet, we are to endure just like Jesus endured. Read that again: He endured the sinners around Him so that He might save them through His obedient life and death, burial, and resurrection. Christians are to endure as we follow in His path, reflecting our Lord and Savior to the fallen world around us.

How do we endure? By looking to Jesus, who finished His race, and brought to the world the forgiveness of sins we endure. Since we believe what the apostles and evangelists have told us about Jesus and have been baptized for the forgiveness of our sins, we can look to Him and endure to the end. Knowing the reasons to believe and having been granted saving faith through the Means of Grace we are equipped to proclaim and defend the faith. We are given that which is needed to endure. This is not about us thinking we can endure in and of ourselves. No, we will trip and fall in that race. Instead, we look to Jesus alone and He grants us that endurance to the end.

It is just incredible, to me, that even though Jesus had to correct and reprove the churches John wrote to in Revelation, that still He encourages and equips us to endure to the end. Apologetics, knowing what you believe and why you believe it, aids in strengthening our fortitude in times of trouble. Never, though, should we be reliant upon the facts given to you in Apologetical studies. Instead, rely upon the one of whom those facts are clearly taught: Jesus Christ of Nazareth who lived, died, and was buried and rose again from the dead according to the Scriptures (cf. 1 Cor 15). He is the One whom you have learned more about through the eyewitness testimonies of the evangelists and apostles who saw, heard, touched, and ate with Him. Jesus is the One whom they tell you about and in whom you believe and have received eternal life. Jude reminds us that in contending for the faith we "build up ourselves in our most holy faith." Therefore, we learn how to defend the faith and by those lessons end up strengthening the faith within.

> Now to Him who is able to keep you from stumbling and to present you blameless before the presence of His glory with great joy, to the only God, our Savior, through Jesus Christ our Lord, be glory, majesty, dominion, and authority, before all time and now and forever. Amen. (Jude 24)

6

Epilogue

My Pastor said to me that "the whole of the Christian life is apologetic" and that is most certainly true. When we live as Christ has taught us, when we proclaim the true faith, when we defend and give reasons why we believe, we are doing Apologetics whether we realize it or not. When we study the Word of God, attend the divine service, partake of the true body and blood of our Lord, we are doing Apologetics. We are saying, "This I believe." When we make confession of sins we are saying, "I believe Jesus died for me for the forgiveness of my sins." Whether Christians recognize it or not, the entire life of the Christian speaks apologetically to the world. When we confess the creeds we are stating an apologetic for the Christian faith. When we embrace the confessions of our faith we are boldly declaring this is what we believe and why. That, my friends, *is* Apologetics.

For many of those who have studied Apologetics, whether at school, through videos, or on their own reading the works of other Christians, none have ever said to me, "This was a waste of time." Instead, God has used the tool of Apologetics to strengthen their faith, helping them grow in their love for God and His Word. They have learned how science, history, and even some aspects of philosophy cohere with God's Word. They have seen that what looks like apparent contradictions or conflicts can be resolved. The result? They become excited to share these truths with others. They have found edification in the proofs of the Christian faith. They have found their own questions answered. When recognizing that we have an objective faith they have kept off their own personal experiences and proclaimed that of the evangelists and apostles.

It is my hope that you have been encouraged to study and then engage in Apologetics because you have seen there are reasons to reason and it is good for you, the Christian, as well as the unbeliever. May God grant you the gifts and graces necessary to give a reason for the hope you have in Christ Jesus.

> Apologetics helps you defend your faith. It does not stop there though.
> Apologetics is also for building you up in the Christian faith.

Bibliography

Almodovar, Nancy A. *A Modern Ninety-Five*. Portland, OR: Resource Publications, n.d.
Anderson, J.N.D. *The World's Religions*. 2nd ed. London: Inter-Varsity Fellowship, 1953.
Anderson, Lanie. "Reasons to Study Apologetics." New Orleans Baptist Theological Seminary, Nov. 26, 2018. https://www.nobts.edu/geauxtherefore/articles/2018/Five-Overlooked-Reasons-to-Study-Apologetics.html.
Bruce, F. F. *The Books and the Parchments: How We Got Our English Bible*. Rev. and updated. Tappan, NJ: F. H. Revell, 1984.
Commission on Worship of the Lutheran Church—Missouri Synod. *Lutheran Service Book*. St. Louis: Concordia, 2006.
Dau, William Hermann Theodore. *Concordia: The Lutheran Confessions—A Reader's Edition of the Book of Concord*. St. Louis: Concordia, 2005.
Evangelical Theological Society. *Evangelical Apologetics*. Camp Hill, PA: Christian Publications, 1996.
Greenleaf, Simon. "Testimony of the Evangelists." UMKS School of Law, n.d. http://law2.umkc.edu/faculty/projects/ftrials/jesus/greenleaf.html.
Kenyon, Frederic. *The Bible and Archaeology*. New York: Harper, 1940.
Latourette, Kenneth Scott. "Christianity Through the Ages." Religion Online, n.d. https://www.religion-online.org/book-chapter/chapter-4-the-initial-five-centuries-of-christianity/.
The Lutheran Study Bible: English Standard Version. St. Louis: Concordia, 2009.
McDowell, Josh. *The New Evidence that Demands a Verdict*. Nashville: T. Nelson, 1999.
Moreland, J. P. *Scaling the Secular City: A Defense of Christianity*. Grand Rapids: Baker Book House, 1987.
Netland, Harold. *Evangelical Apologetics*. Camp Hill, PA: Christian Publications, 1996.
Pelikan, Jarislov. "If Christ Is Risen, Nothing Else Matters." Phoenix Seminary, April 12, 2020. https://ps.edu/if-christ-is-risen-nothing-else-matters/.
———,ed. *Luther's Works*. Vol. 40. St. Louis: Concordia, 1955–86.

BIBLIOGRAPHY

Smith, William, Dr. "Canon of Scripture, The." *Smith's Bible Dictionary*. 1901. https://www.biblestudytools.com/dictionary/canon-of-scripture-the/.

Torrey, R. A. *Our Bible: How We Got It and Ten Reasons Why I Believe the Bible Is the Word of God*. Colportage Library ed., 64. Chicago: Bible Institute Colportage Association, 1898.

Treasury of Daily Prayer. St. Louis: Concordia, 2008.

Warwick, John Montgomery. *Faith Founded on Fact: Essays in Evidential Apologetics*. Nashville: T. Nelson, 1978.

www.ingramcontent.com/pod-product-compliance
Lightning Source LLC
Chambersburg PA
CBHW061511040426
42450CB00008B/1566